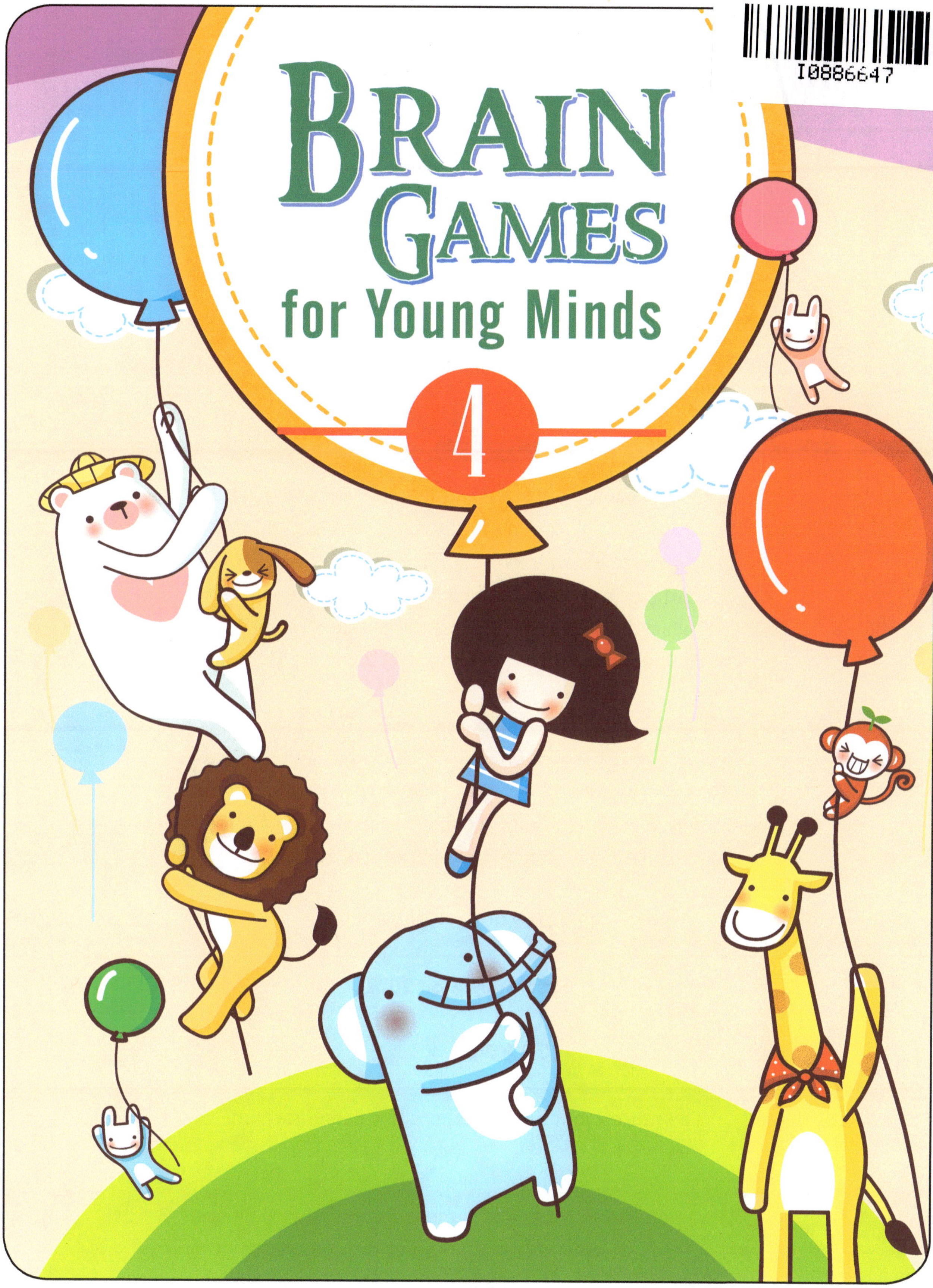

MOONSTONE

Published in Moonstone
by Rupa Publications India Pvt. Ltd 2022
7/16, Ansari Road, Daryaganj
New Delhi 110002

Sales centres:
Allahabad Bengaluru Chennai
Hyderabad Jaipur Kathmandu
Kolkata Mumbai

ISBN: - 978-93-5520-880-4

First impression 2022

10 9 8 7 6 5 4 3 2 1

1. Match It

Match the animals to their natural habitats.

1. 

Desert

2. 

Rainforest

3. 

Ocean

4. 

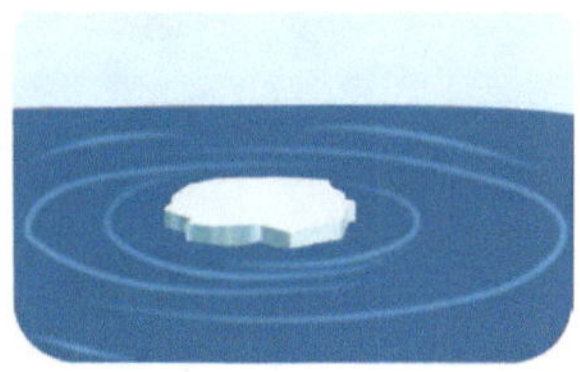

Polar Region

5. 

Lake

6. 

Grassland

2. Word Search

Read the clues and find the missing words in the word search below.

J	J	A	R	T	G	R	Y	R	D
Y	V	L	J	H	B	R	E	A	W
V	S	R	V	A	P	E	U	D	U
X	M	C	Z	N	S	S	Q	I	B
P	O	T	N	D	N	T	E	O	P
A	K	O	I	I	G	A	N	A	U
R	I	U	F	C	R	U	T	C	I
K	N	C	E	A	V	R	R	T	E
I	G	H	H	P	I	A	Y	I	P
N	L	N	Y	P	Q	N	D	V	M
G	N	C	K	E	C	T	O	E	S
E	X	I	T	D	C	X	M	L	V

1. 

No S______________

2. 

Do not T____________

3. 

No P______________

4. 

R______________

5. 

H______________

6. 

Fire E______________

7. 

R ______________

8. 

No E______________

3. Animal Produce

Look at the groups of items given below. Write the name of the animal from which we get the given food items.

1. 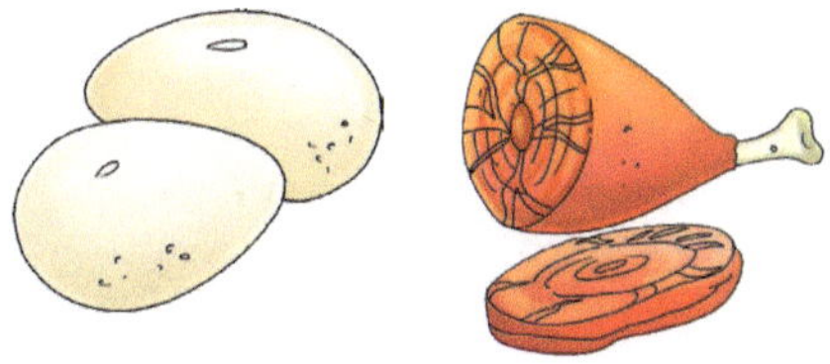

2. 

3. 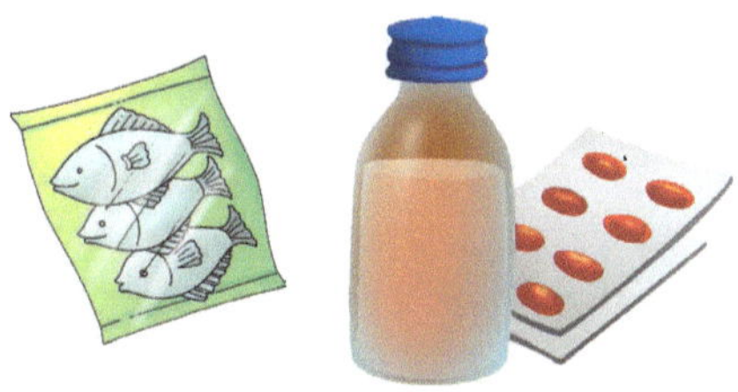

4. 

5. 

4. Foody Crossword

Solve the riddles and name the fruits and vegetables.

Across (Fruits)

2. I am brown and thorny from outside but yellow and sweet inside.

3. I am both a colour and a fruit. I am also the brother of lemon

6. I wear a red robe with a stone at the centre.

8. I am juicy with yellow flesh and also the name of a colour. There is a stone in my heart.

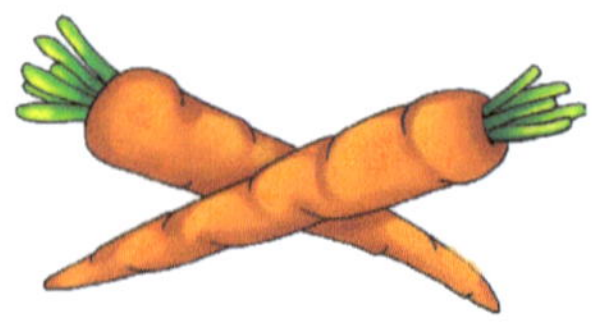

Down (Vegetables)

1. I can make people cry when they cut me.

4. I am a close relative of onions covered in white. I add flavour to your food but called as a stinking rose.

5. I am small, green and round hidden in my pods.

7. I have green hair with a long body. I grow under the ground in dark.

5. Smart Seasons

Identify and name the seasons. Match them with the related objects.

Winter	Summer	Rainy

6. Pollutants

Find the names of eight major pollutants in the word search and write them below.

X	N	Z	C	H	E	M	I	C	A	L
S	U	I	P	W	O	X	W	T	K	I
I	C	H	Z	Q	Q	G	A	S	U	T
O	L	I	C	K	E	S	B	H	Q	T
R	E	F	T	K	M	T	P	Y	N	E
V	A	S	N	R	J	D	K	O	A	R
M	R	X	X	H	Q	T	L	X	J	P
T	A	U	T	O	M	O	B	I	L	E
V	P	E	S	T	I	C	I	D	E	K
G	U	U	O	D	R	S	T	K	S	S
Y	S	S	E	W	A	G	E	F	O	J
R	X	S	Z	J	L	L	O	P	Q	M
I	N	D	U	S	T	R	I	E	S	Q
J	F	O	S	S	I	L	F	U	E	L

7. Correct the Sequence

Mark the images from 1 to 6 to show the process of growing a plant in the correct order. Also, name them with the help of clue box.

Sapling	Watering
Sowing seeds	Plant
Put in sunlight	Digging soil

8. Growing Patterns

The following patterns are growing rapidly. Complete them according to the given growth pattern.

1.

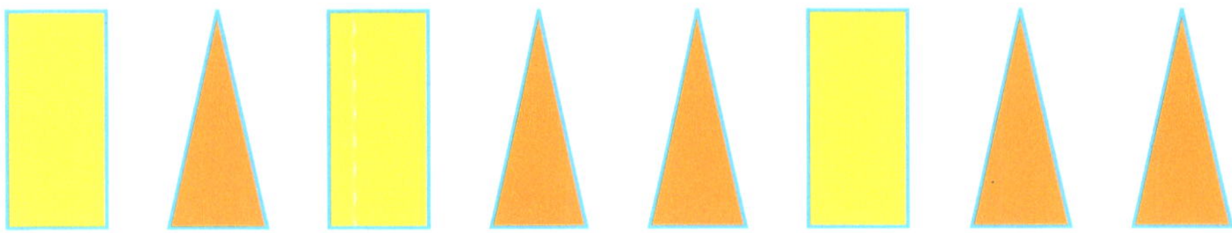 ______ ______

2.

 ______ ______

3.

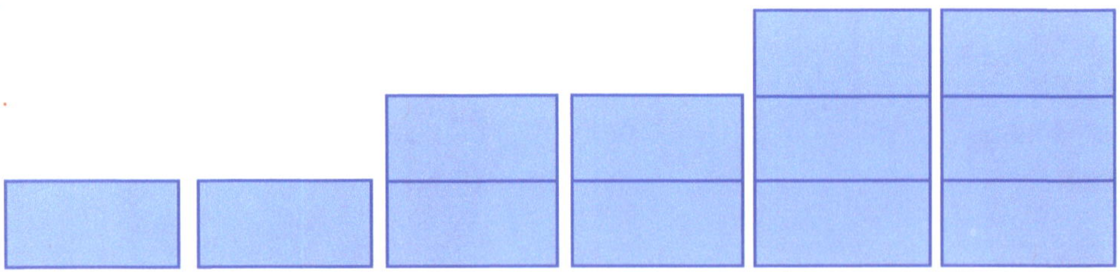 ______ ______

4.

 ______ ______

5.

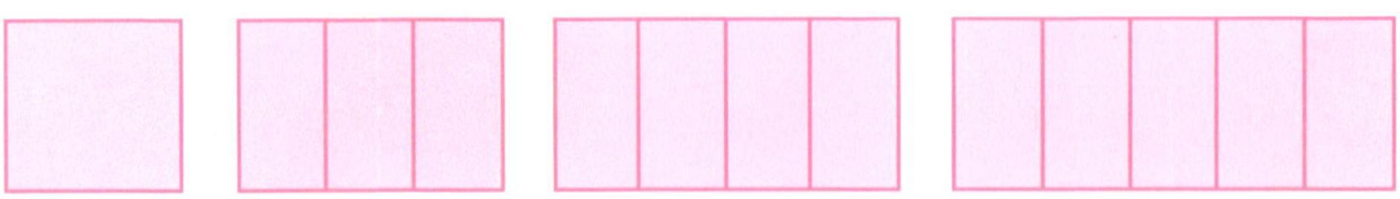 ______ ______

6.

 ______ ______

9. Plants as Givers

We get many things from plants. Find their names in the word search and write them below.

S	L	X	K	I	W	I	S	T	B
U	C	A	R	R	O	T	P	A	Y
N	C	P	U	G	G	G	I	P	C
F	V	P	C	W	Z	Q	N	M	O
L	E	L	I	D	G	J	A	U	T
O	W	E	W	B	D	U	C	S	T
W	H	R	E	G	D	T	H	T	O
E	E	I	R	K	A	E	E	A	N
R	A	C	U	T	Q	I	P	R	O
B	T	E	K	H	Z	Z	U	D	S

Fruits ________________ ________________

Vegetables ________________ ________________

Fibres ________________ ________________

Oils ________________ ________________

Cereals ________________ ________________

10. Life of a Frog

Name the different stages in the life cycle of a frog. Complete the sentences by writing the features of a frog.

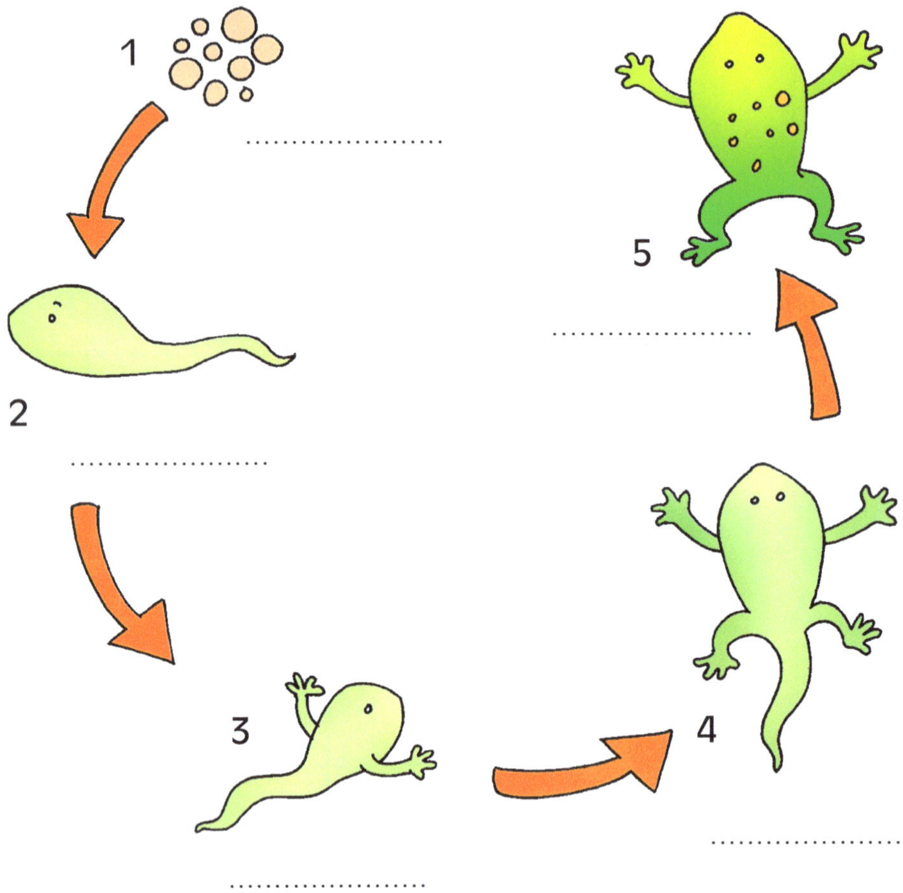

6. Frogs breathe through their ____________________.

7. Frogs can live on ____________________ and in ____________________.

8. Frogs have ____________________ feet.

9. Frogs have a ____________________ tongue.

skin	long
land, water	webbed

11. Speller's Zone

Two different spellings of a single word are given below. Identify the correct one.

1.	Calendar	Calender
2.	Column	Colamn
3.	Arguement	Argument
4.	Futher	Further
5.	Lollipop	Lolypop
6.	Interupt	Interrupt
7.	Tommorrow	Tomorrow
8.	Publicly	Publically

12. Name It

Match the people with their tools and name the tools with the help of clue box.

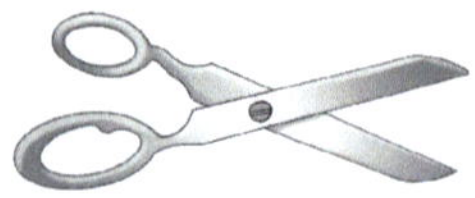

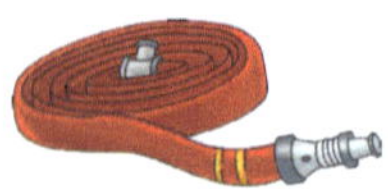

Scissor	Brush	Stationery
Utensils	Water hose	Tools

13. Wild Lifestyle

Match the animals with their sound and food.

Trumpet		Grass
Squeak		Deer
Roar		Cheese
Neigh		Sugarcane
Hiss		Mouse
Moo		Grass

14. My Senses

Fill in the blanks and complete the poem.

________ the bells ringing,
the dogs bark, the birds sing,
________ the bells ringing.

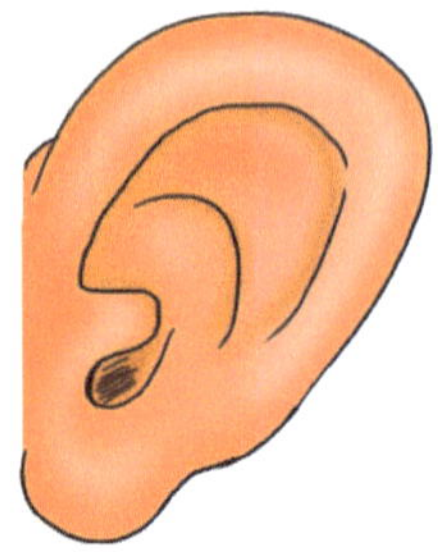

________the flowers dancing,
The bright moon, the twinkling stars,
________ the flower dancing.

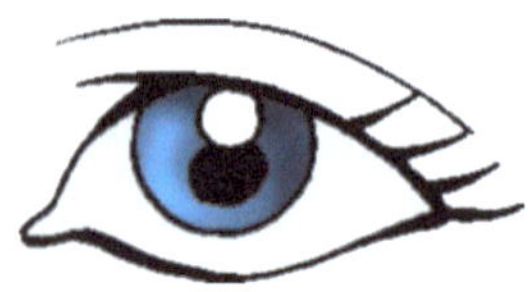

________ the fresh air,
The pretty flowers, the baked bread,
________ the fresh air.

________ the sweet candy,
The sour lemon, the salty chips,
________ the sweet candy.

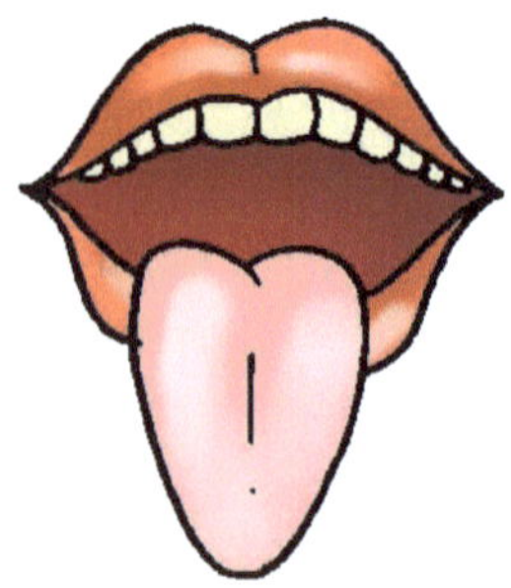

________ the soft grass,
The cold ice, the rough wall,
________ the soft grass.

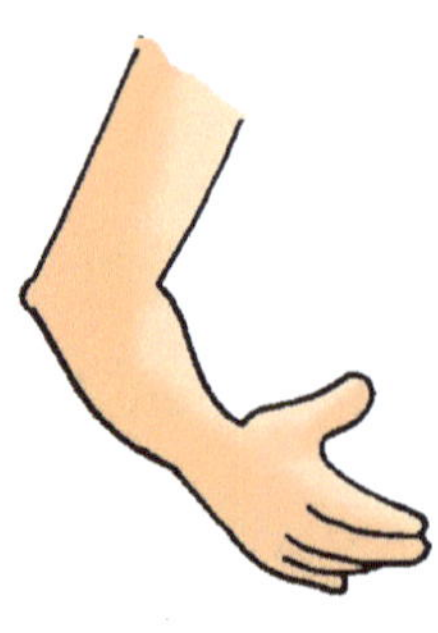

15. Mirror Image

Find the correct mirror image of each of the following.

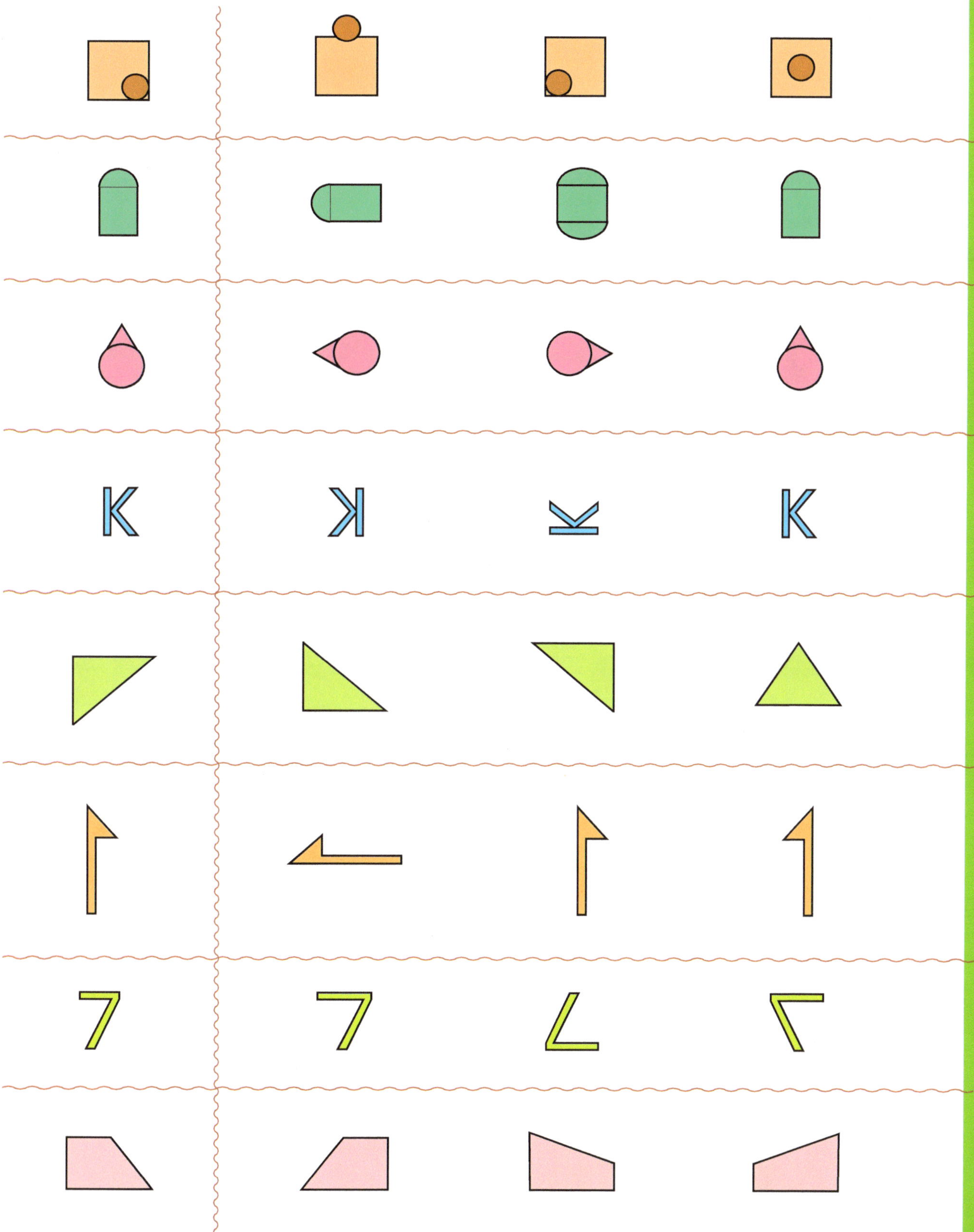

16. Take Me Home

We also make homes for some animals. Identify the man-made homes of the given animals.

1. 

Coop

2. 

Cage

3. 

Stable

4. 

Shed

5. 

Kennel

6. 

Fish Bowl

17. Tricky Phrases

Solve the clues and guess the phrases.

1. SIT
FENCE

....

2. 

....

3. IsockT

....

4. 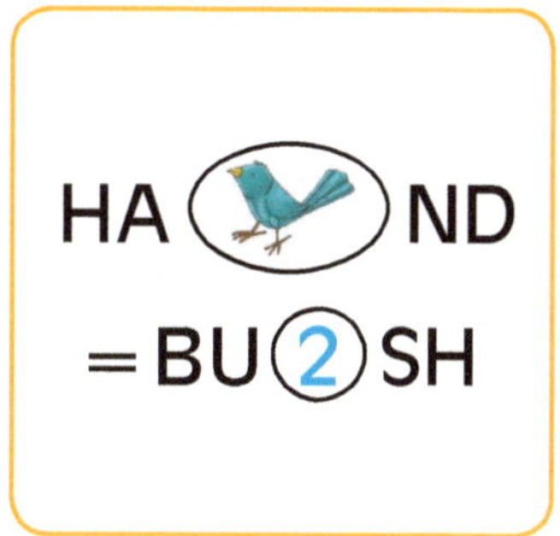

....

5. laugh laugh
laugh laugh
laugh laugh
laugh laugh

....

6. 

....

7. 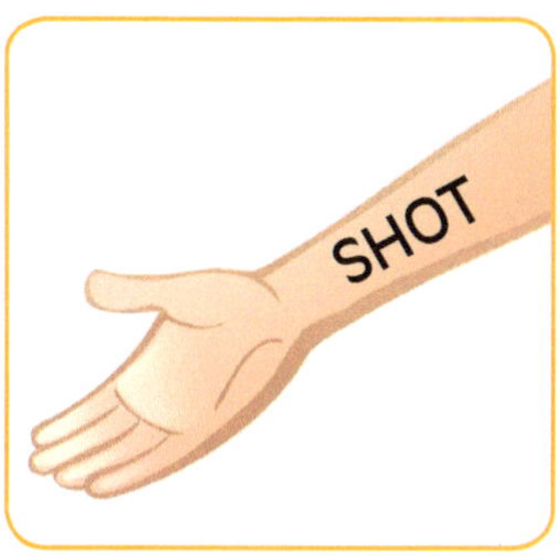

....

8. Give Give
Give Give
Get Get
Get Get

....

18. Find the Sign

Identify the road signs and complete the sentences given with each sign.

1. It tells the vehicles to S_ _ _.

2. It allows the pedestrians to w_ _ _.

3. Pedestrians can c _ _ _ _ the road from here.

4. It allows to take a l _ _ _ t _ _ _.

5. It p _ _ _ _ _ _ _ _ us to move forward.

6. It allows to take a U-_ _ _ _.

7. It shows that a r _ _ _ _ _ _ _ _ _ is going to come.

left turn	roundabout		stop
cross	walk	u-turn	prohibits

19. Bird Riddles

Solve the riddles and name the birds.

1. I am the coolest bird. I fly in water instead of flying in the air.

P						

2. I am the largest living bird. I cannot fly but I can kick my enemies.

O						

3. My wife is a hen. My child is a chick. I wake you up in the morning.

C			

4. I sleep during day and wake up at night. I can turn my neck all way round.

O		

5. I am colourful with a strong and curved bill. Seeds are my favourite food.

P					

6. I have a sharp beak and claws. I eat only meat and I can fly up high.

E				

20. Unscramble the Words

Identify the weather symbols and write their names.

DIWYN ________________

UERTNH ________________

YUCOLD ________________

NUNYS ________________

ANRIY ________________

WNOYS ________________

ATPRLY ODYCLU ________________

21. Pollution Panic

Complete the sentences given below and identify the sources of pollution.

1. Old vehicles give out __ __o__e which causes air pollution.

2. Smoke from __a__ __ o __ ie__ is a cause of air pollution.

3. Playing loud __ u__ i __ creates noise pollution.

4. Dumping __ a __ __ e into rivers causes water pollution.

5. __ e __ o __ e __ __ a __ io __ is the major cause of soil erosion.

6. __ __ e __ i __ als and waste products affect the quality of fertile land.

7. Oil __ __ i __ __ __ into seas is the cause of death of a lot of marine animals.

waste	music	spills	smoke
chemicals	factories		Deforestation

22. Water Cycle

Name the different steps of water cycle using the clues given below.

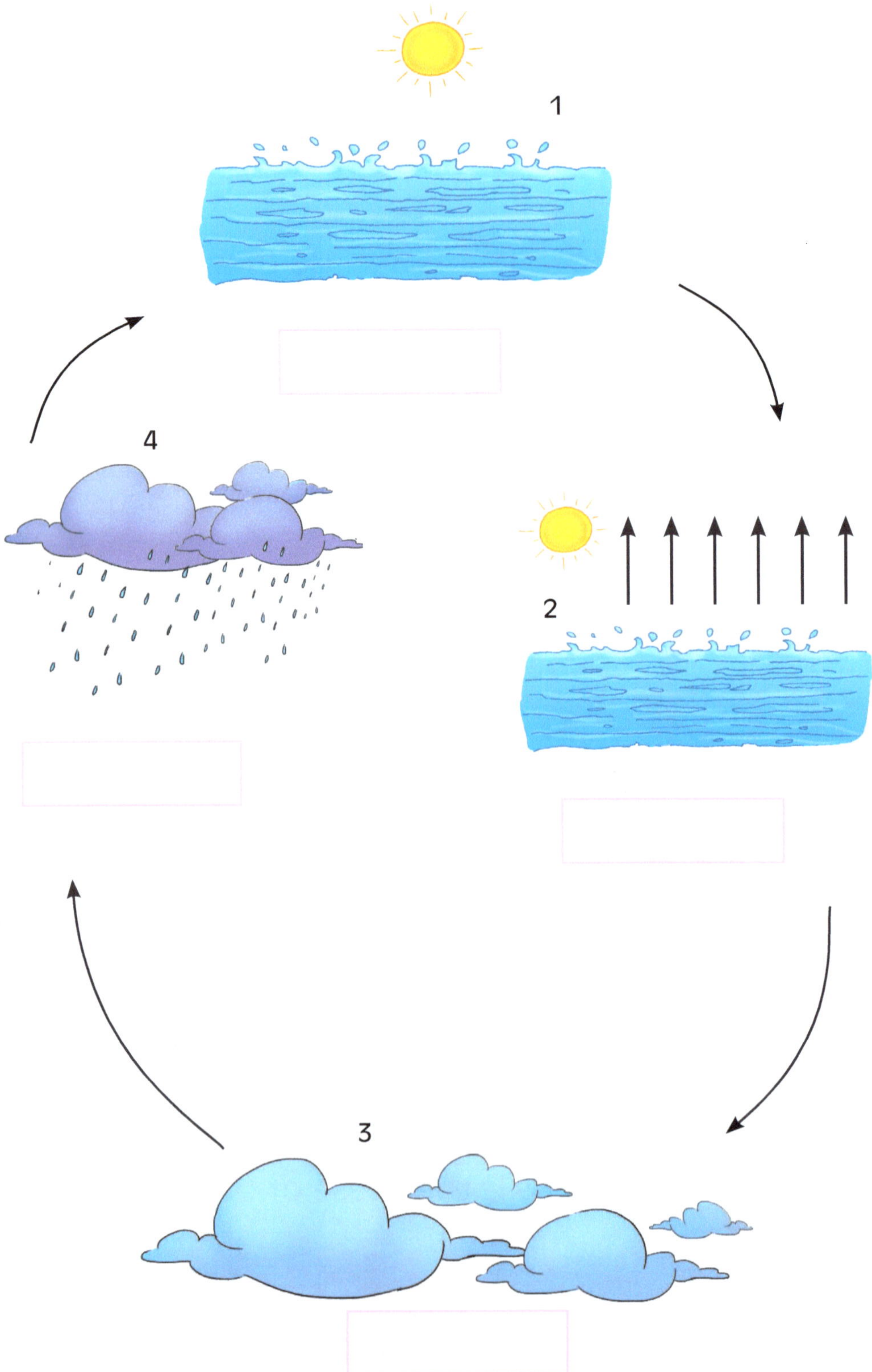

Rainfall	Condensation
Sun Shines	Evaporation

23. Finish the Patterns

Choose the symbol that should come next.

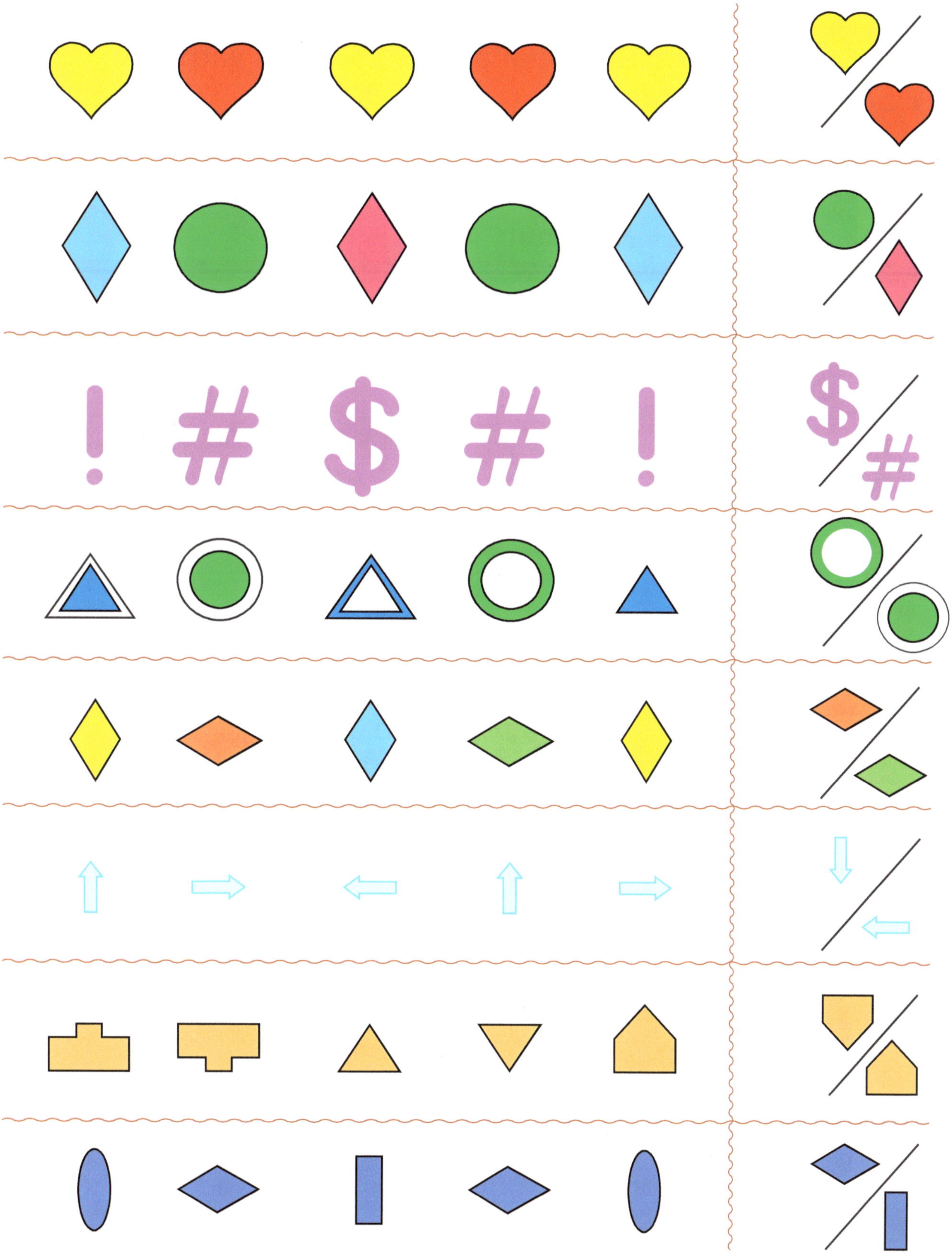

24. Being a Butterfly

Complete the sentence given below using words from the clue box.

1. 

The life of a butterfly starts with an ________.

Most butterflies lay their eggs on the ______ of a plant.

2. 

A ________ hatches out of the egg. They eat their own ________.

3. 

An adult caterpillar changes into a _______ which is also called as chrysalis.

4. 

The __________ breaks the pupa shell and emerges out.

eggshell	pupa	butterfly
caterpillar	leaves	egg

25. Hard to Spell

Write the vowels 'e' and 'i' in the correct order to complete the words.

1. W __ __ rd
6. For __ __ gn
2. S __ __ ge
7. Bel __ __ ve
3. Rec __ __ ve
8. Ach __ __ ve
4. P __ __ ce
9. H __ __ ght
5. Fr __ __ nd
10. Sc __ __ nce

26. Who Am I?

Read the clue and identify the person. Write their names in the given space.

1. I cook food for people.

I am a ____

2. I give you medicine to treat your sickness.

I am a ____

3. I fix leaking taps and water pipes.

I am a ____

4. I teach children in a school.

I am a ____

5. I guard the country and protect the people from enemies.

I am a ____

soldier	teacher	doctor
plumber	chef	

27. Winter Wonderland

The picture below shows the winter season. Circle the children who are wearing winter clothes.

Circle the clothes that you wear in winter.

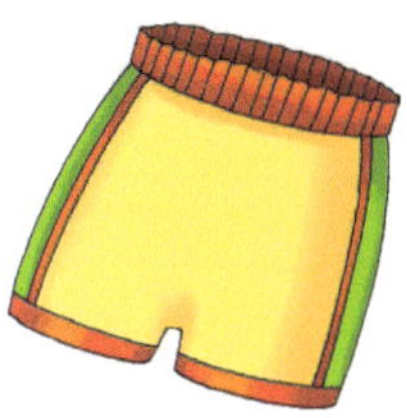
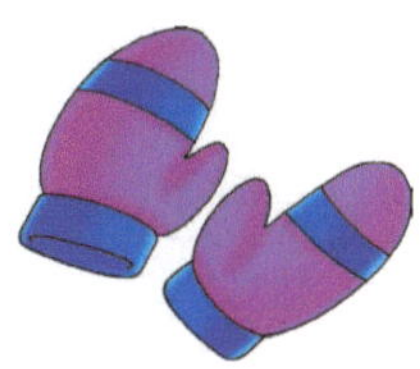

28. Identify Shapes

Circle the shapes which are polygons.

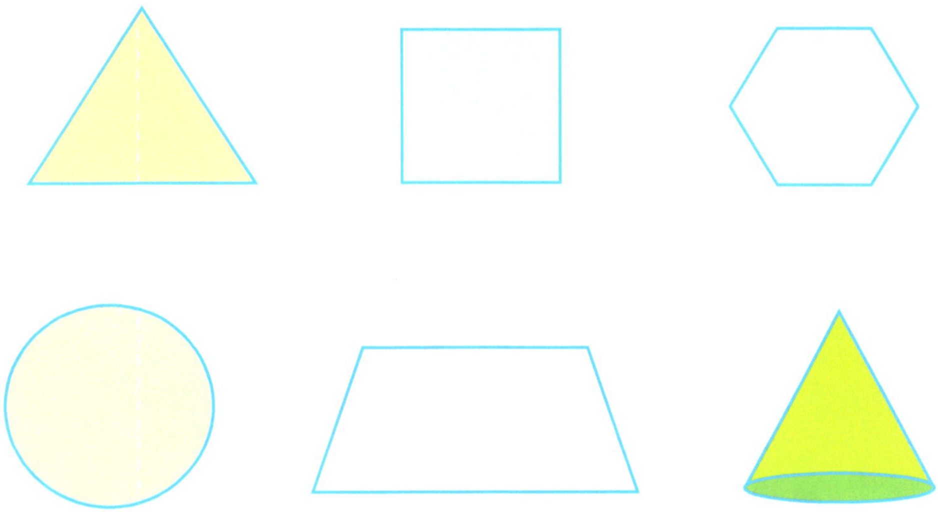

Circle the shapes which are not polygons.

29. Find It

Find the correct mirror image of each of the following.

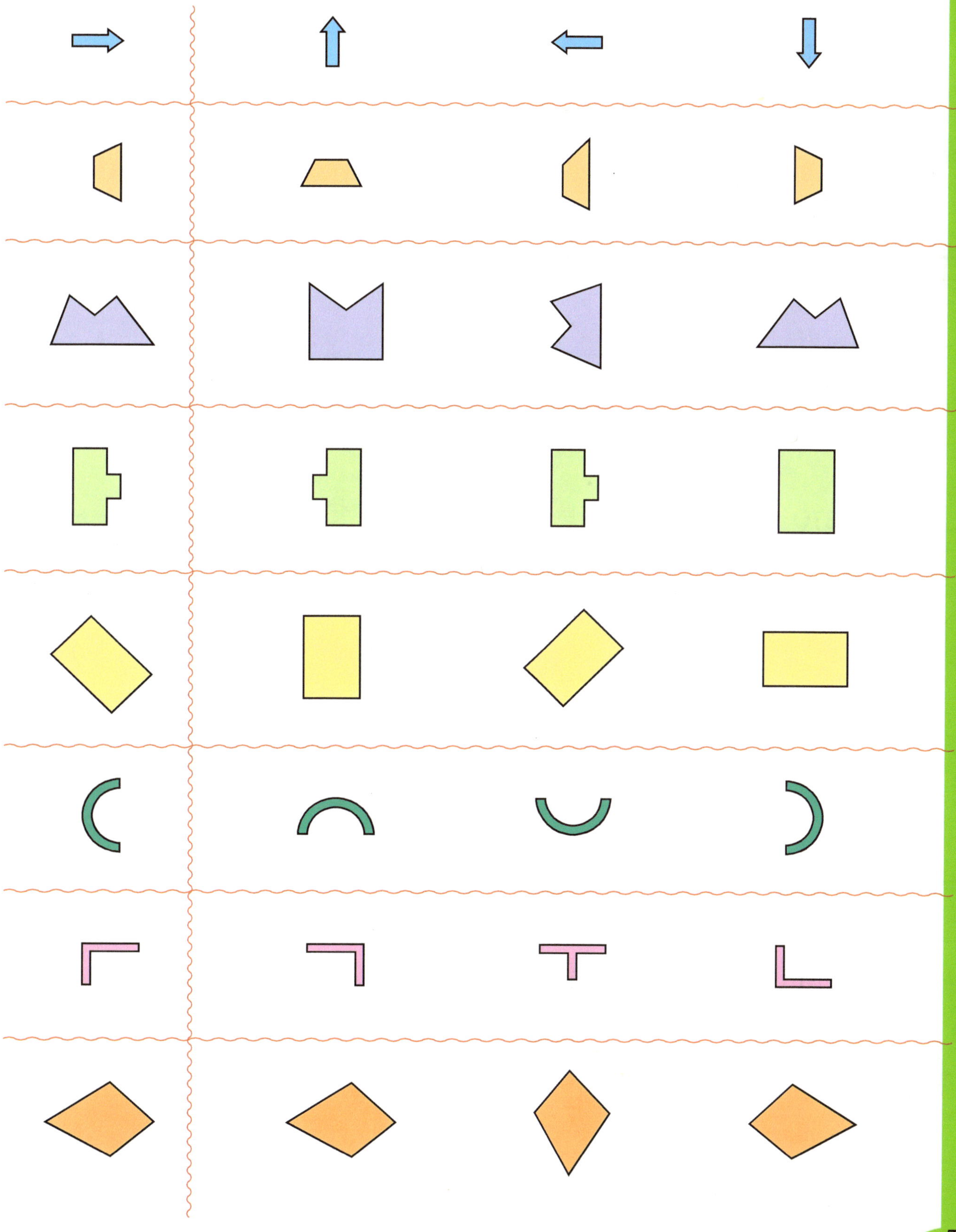

30. Where Are They?

Unscramble the letters given below and form the location words.

1. EEBTWNE

2. OBLWE

3. NSIIDE

4. TMOBTO

5. BOEVA

6. EVOR

7. NEBHDI

8. DRNEU

31. Leaf Maze

Mr. Caterpillar is at the end of the leaf. Help it reach Ms. Ant by crossing the maze

32. Guess the Animal

Guess the animal in each of the following riddle and write its name.

1. I belong to the family of mongoose. I live in large underground tunnels.

2. I am a small creature with my house on my back. I crawl through my way.

3. I am red and clever with a bushy tail. I live in the forest.

4. I live in the coldest water and ice. My coat keeps me warm and dry.

5. I am a big cat with sharp eyes. My black and yellow strips help me to hide.

6. I am the largest land animal with a big grey body and a trunk.

Fox	Elephant	Meerkat
Polar bear	Tiger	Snail

33. Rainy Season

The picture below shows the rainy season. Mark the objects which you see during rainy season.

Match the objects to their names.

Gumboots
Rainbow
Raincoat
Umbrella

34. Circle It

Circle the animals that can be domesticated.

Circle the animals that can fly.

35. Word Scramble

Unscramble the letters and write the action words which begin with the letter 's'.

1. GWSIN →
2. SEZNEE →
3. RBUCS →
4. HSOUT →
5. ATKSE →
6. NDTSA →
7. WISM →
8. DISLE →

36. Things We Use

People make different things for us. Match the people to the things they make.

37. Double It

Identify the pictures and fill in the blanks with the correct double consonants.

Bu__ __ on

Te __ __ y

Pu __ __ y

Mu __ __ in

Pi __ __ ow

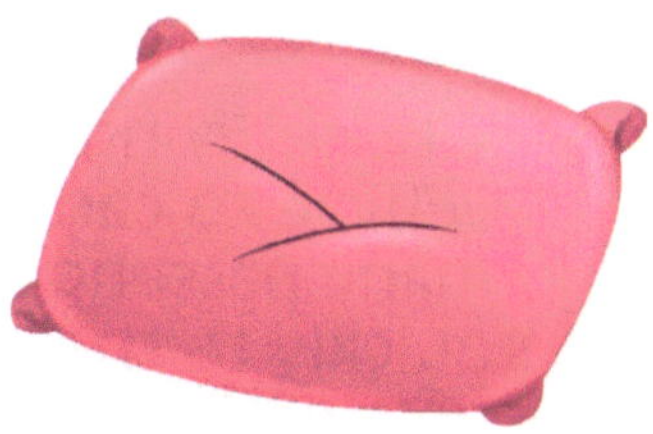

Ca __ __ot

38. Ride It

Read the clues and find the names of the vehicles.

Across:

2. A large road vehicle to carry passengers.
5. A large flying vehicle to carry many passengers quickly to their destination.
7. A two wheeler that you ride by pushing pedals.
8. A vehicle used to travel in space.

Down:

1. A ship that travels underwater.
3. A large water vehicle that carries people and goods.
4. A vehicle for travelling over snow or ice.
6. A personal vehicle with four wheels with an engine.
9. A vehicle with many coaches which run on tracks.

39. Use the Bin

Match each waste product to the correct dustbin.

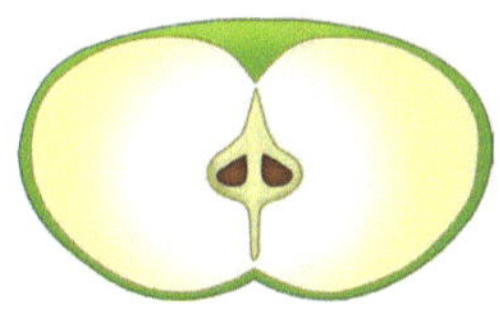

Compost Recycle Reuse

40. Find the Path

Help Mr. Bunny to cross the maze and reach the carrot.

41. Race Time

The given animals have participated in a race. Help them win the race by completing the patterns.

42. Visiting Places

Unscramble the letters given below and find the names of the places.

1. LTEHO

2. IRRYALB

3. CSHLOO

4. TKEAMR

5. USUMEM

6. KABN

7. IOPSATHL

8. AKRP

43. Find the Pattern

Find the mirror image of the following letters.

44. Word Clues

Solve the clues to find the letters. Use the letter found to complete the sentence.

1. It is in  but not in ROW.

2. It is in 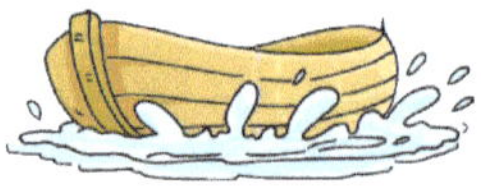 but not in BAT.

3. It is in  but not in SON.

4. It is in  but not in NOSE.

5. It is in 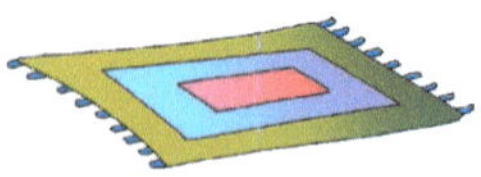 but not in TOM.

6. It is in  but not in TIRE.

7. It is in  but not in GAG.

Have _ _ _ _ _ _ _ and be kind.

45. What's that Animal?

Unscramble the words and form an animal name.

1. FLOW

2. BRAZE

3. HEAR

4. SHORE

5. BARE

6. LOW

7. REED

8. CHAINED

46. Prefix Time

Use the picture clues to add the prefix and make the words.

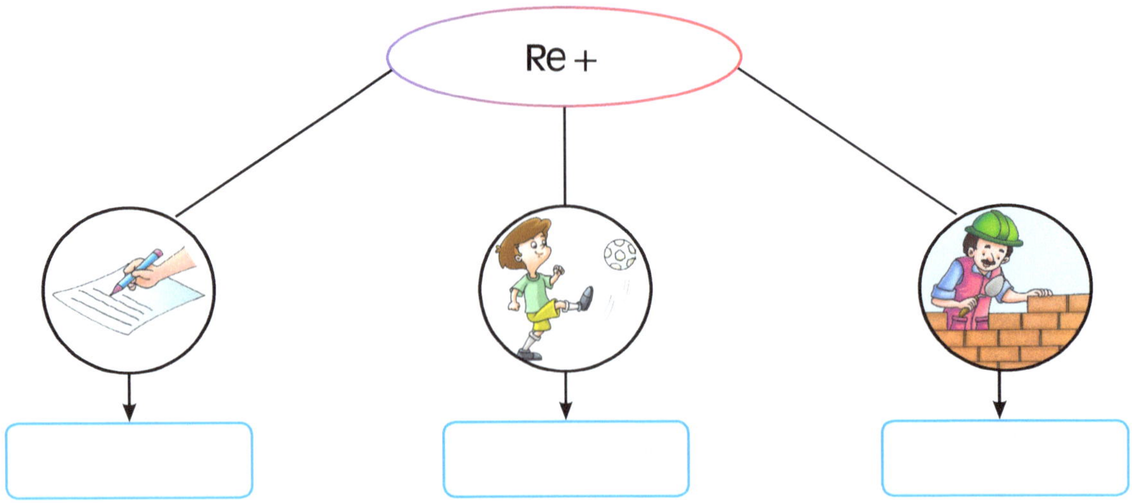

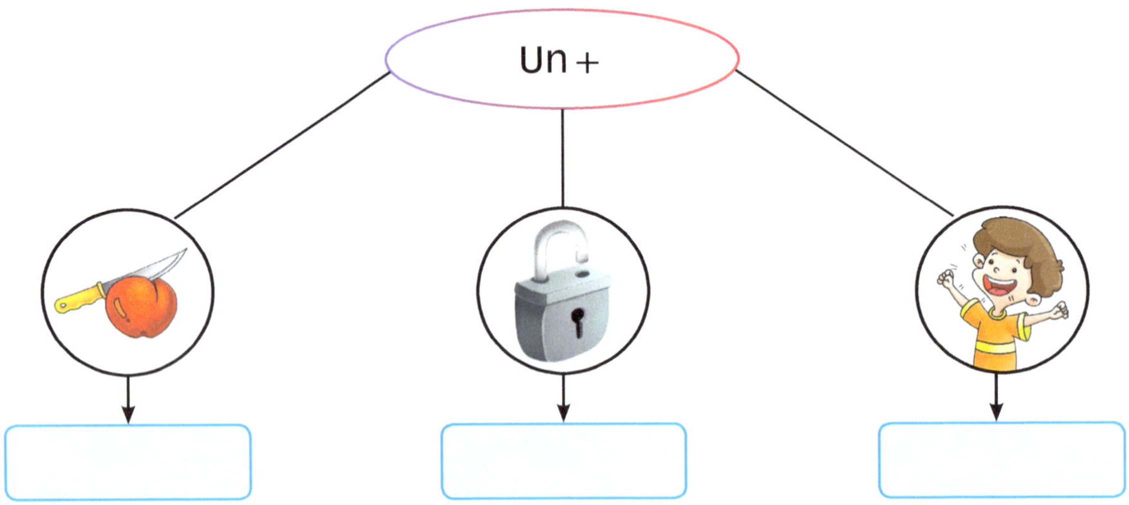

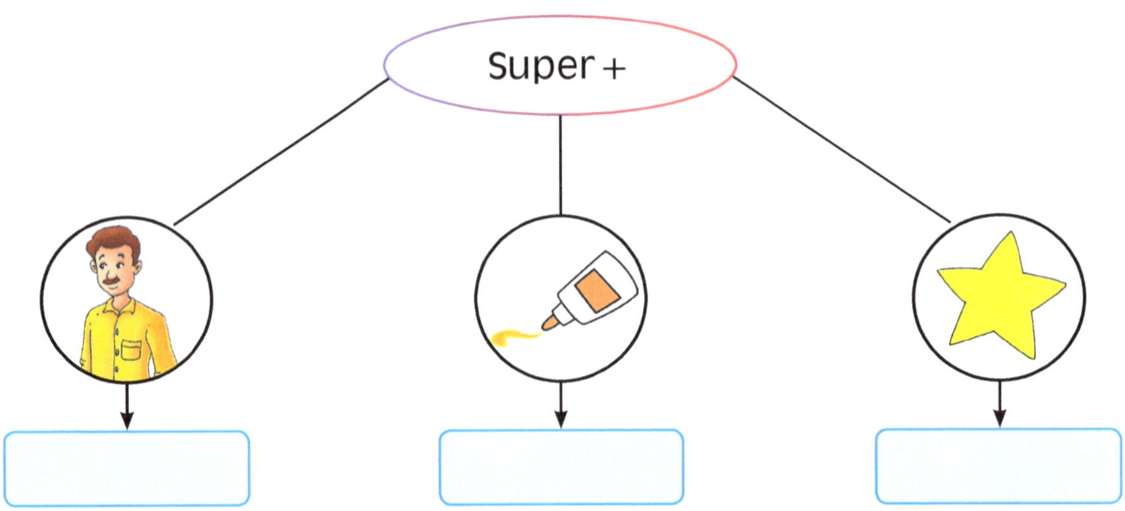

47. Crazy Colours

Pictures given in the first column rhyme with a colour. Match them to the correct colour.

Z

48. Bake a Cake

Choose the words from the box below to complete the story.

cake	waist	grapes	plate
tray	apron	bake	rainy

1. Today is a __________________ day.

2. Mary wants to bake a fruit __________________.

3. She puts on the __________________ around her __________________.

4. She lets the cake in oven to __________________ it.

5. She adds berries and __________________ to the cake.

6. Mary took a piece of cake in a __________________.

7. She kept the rest of the cake in a __________________.

49. Finding Sounds

Complete each word with a digraph from the box. Draw a line from the word to its picture.

ch	ph	sh	th	wh	ck	ng

1. __ __ eel

2. Ki __ __

3. Tee __ __

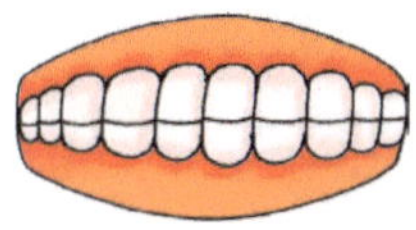

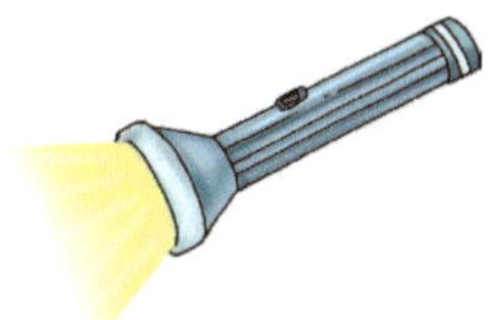

4. Tor __ __

5. __ __ eep

6. Du __ __

7. __ __ one

50. Word Fusion

Name the pictures and fuse them with the given words to form new words.

1. LUNCH + 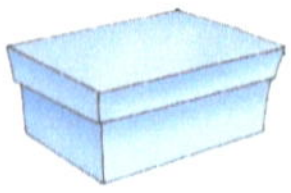 =

2.  + BOW =

3. LIGHT +  =

4.  + BOWL =

5. 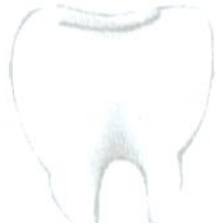 + BRUSH =

6. POP +  =

7.  + FLOWER =

51. Word Find

Solve the clues to find the letters. Use the letters found to complete the sentence.

1. Present in  but absent in MUD.

2. Present in 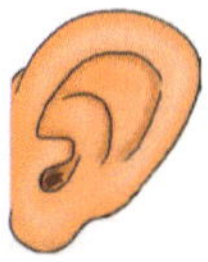 but absent in ARM.

3. Present in  but absent in COT.

4. Present in  but absent in BEE.

5. Present in  but absent in ACE.

6. Present in  but absent in APE.

7. Present in  but absent in BAN.

exercises the brain.

52. Suffix Time

Use the picture clues to add the suffix and make the words.

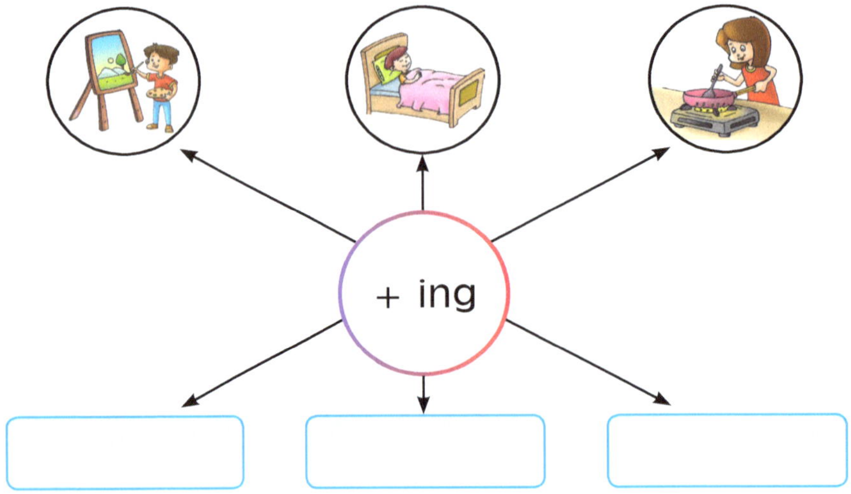

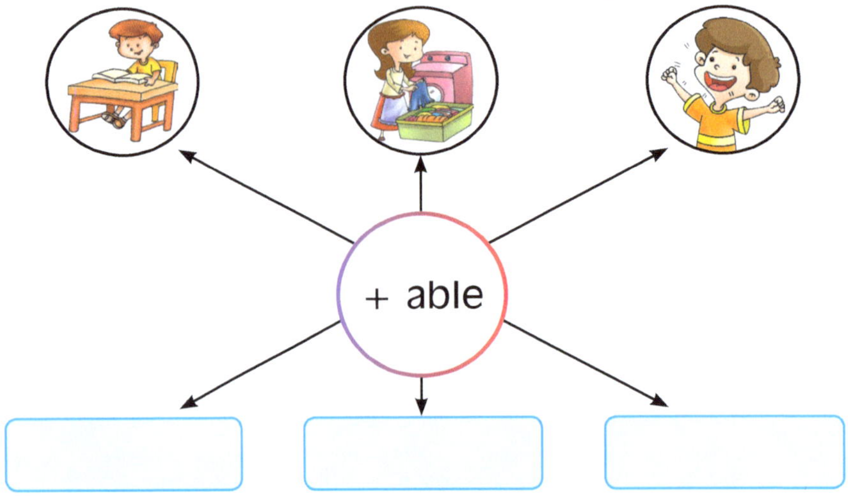

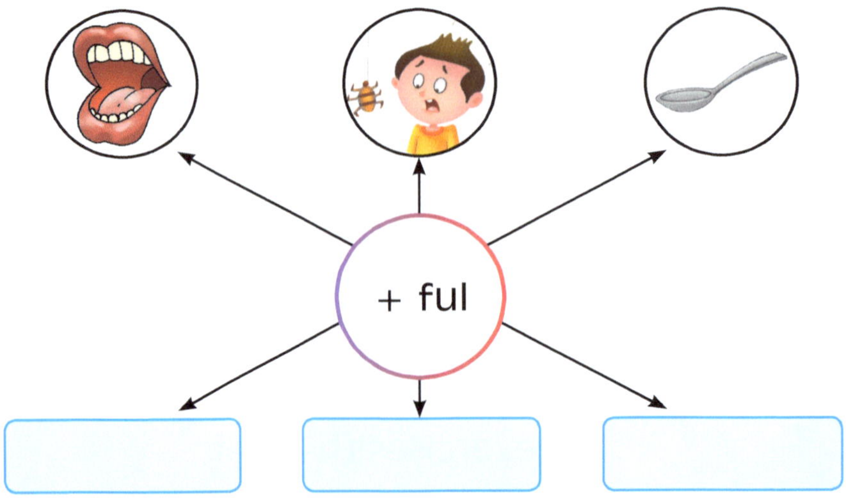

53. Rhyme Time

Match the clothes to the pictures with which they rhyme.

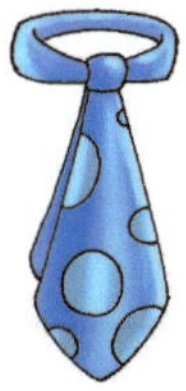

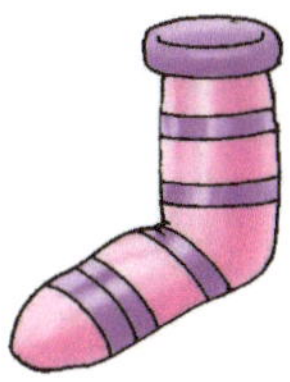

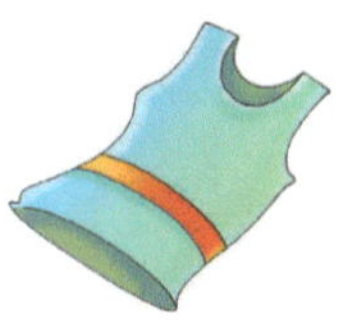

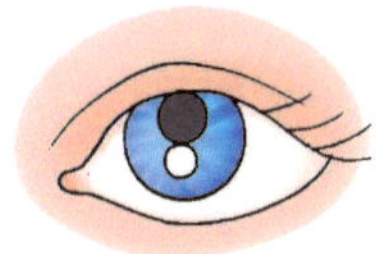

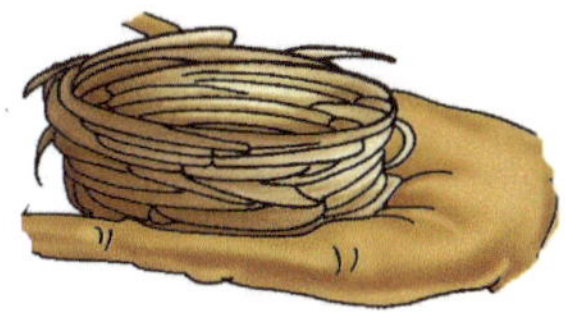
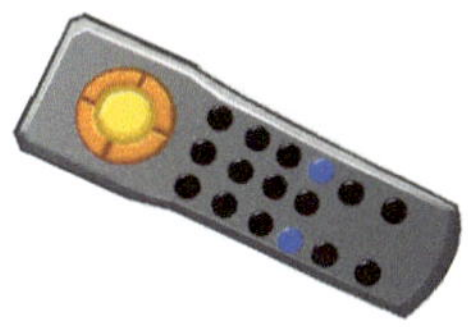

54. Vowel Sounds

Circle the pictures having long vowel sounds with red colour and circle the pictures having short vowel sounds with yellow colour.

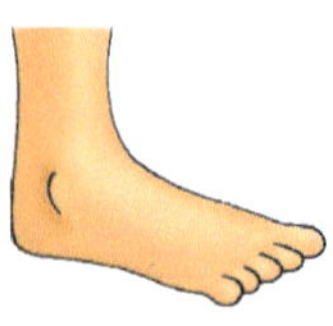

55. Consonant Cluster

Join the pictures to the sounds they begin with.

1. 
2. 
3. 
4. 
5. 
6. 
7. 

RO

CL

CL

IN

SW

PL

BL

56. Match-Making

Match the words to make a common compound word.

Butter	Ball
Cup	Book
Gold	Mill
Base	Ring
Note	Pot
Ear	Fly
Snow	Crow
Tea	Cake
Wind	Fish
Scare	Man

57. Name It

Unscramble the words and form action words.

1. ABET
2. ACRES
3. TAP
4. PLEASE
5. BRAG
6. CALLER
7. LIPS
8. SHEAR

58. Word Mania

Solve the clues to find the letters. Use the letters found to complete the sentence.

1. Find it in  but not in TEN.

2. Find it in  but not in HELL.

3. Find it in 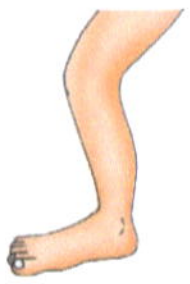 but not in LOG.

4. Find it in  but not in NOTE.

5. Find it in  but not in DIG.

6. Find it in  but not in COB.

7. Find it in  but not in PIN.

The word is

59. In a Fix

Use the picture clues to find the hidden words and their prefix or suffix.

1.  + ( -f) = Childish

2. ( -b) + ( -cy) =

3. ( -g) +  =

4.  + ( -Ke) =

5.  + ( -Sw) =

6. ( -nt) + 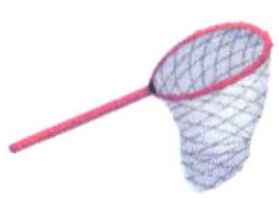 =

7. ( -J) + ( -jel) =

8.  + ( -k) =

60. Foody Fun

Match the fruits to the objects that rhyme with them.

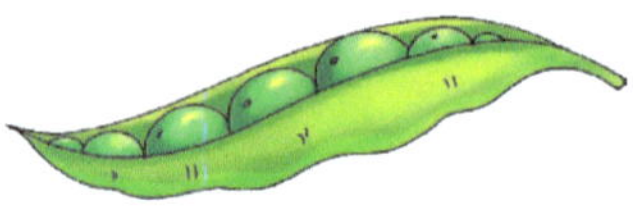

61. Magic Maze

Follow the words with long 'i' vowel sound and help the bee reach its hive.

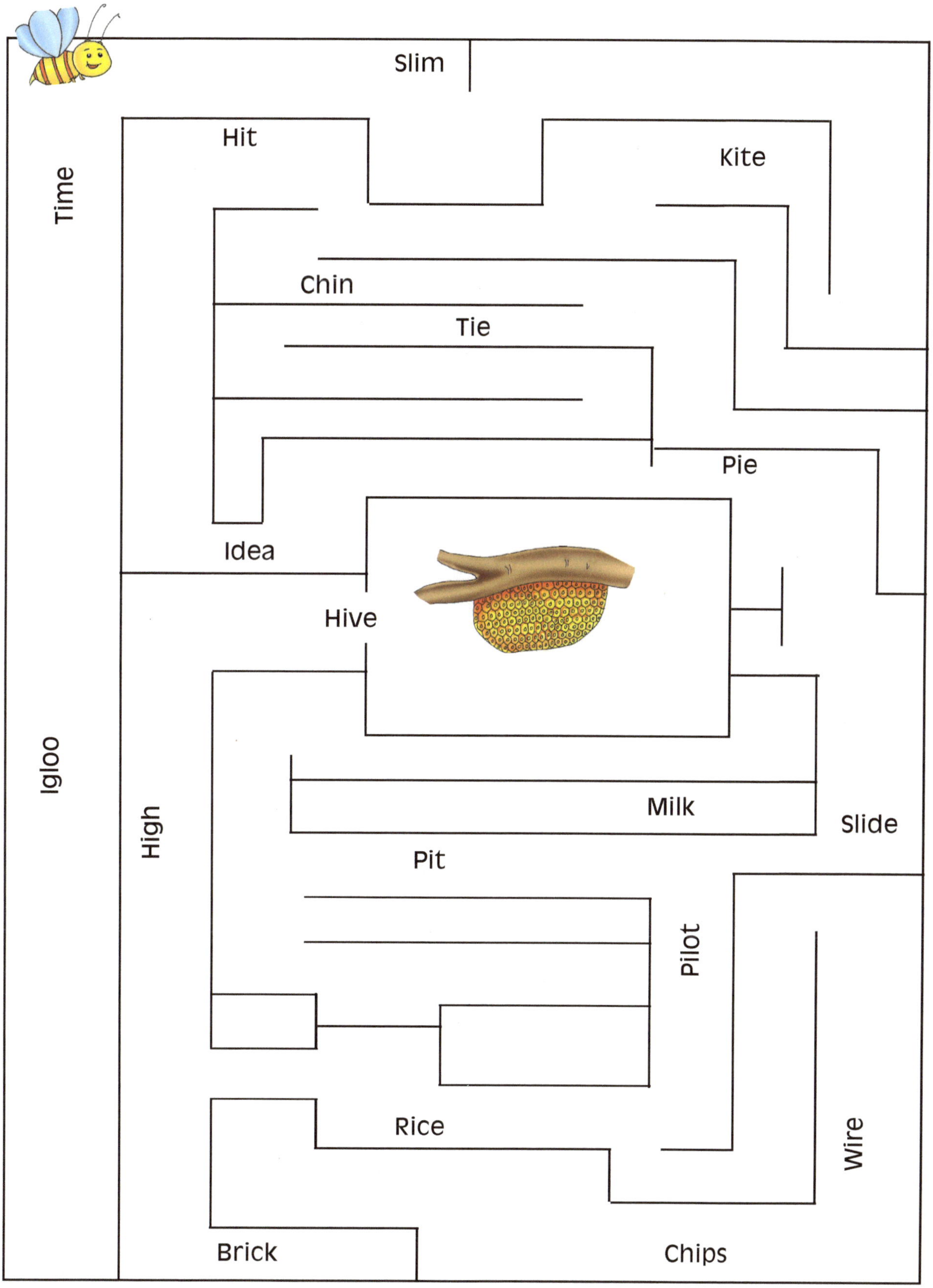

62. Pick the Sound

Name the pictures shown below and put a tick on the correct blend sound.

1.		dr	gr	br
2.		tr	dr	pr
3.		fr	cr	pr
4.		br	dr	gr
5.		fr	cr	dr
6.		fr	tr	pr
7.		pr	dr	tr

63. Guess the Word

Fill the blanks using the correct words.

1. The bee is sitting on a ________________ . flower flour

2. She was looking ____________________ . pail pale

3. The bucket has a __________________ in it. whole hole

4. She tied the ____________________ . knot not

5. ________________ is an alloy. Steal Steel

6. The lion killed a ______________________ . deer dear

7. The mouse has a thin __________________ . tail tale

64. Name the Group

Name the collective noun which you can use for the following animal groups.

1.  ____________

2.  ____________

3.  ____________

4.  ____________

5.  ____________

6.  ____________

7.  ____________

8.  ____________

Pride	Flock	Herd	Swarm
Pack	School	Colony	Litter

65. Pick One

Circle the words with the correct spelling of the name of the objects.

1.

Robote | Robot

2.

Frog | Froog

3.

Boan | Bone

4.

Soap | Sope

5.

Log | Loge

6.

Mope | Mop

66. Circle It

Out of the options given, which picture matches the consonant sound in the middle?

1. 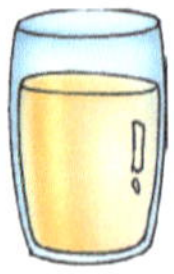 ft 

2.  nt 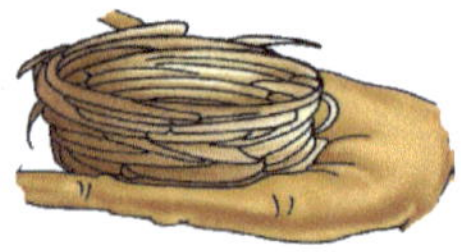

3.  mp 

4.  nk 

5. 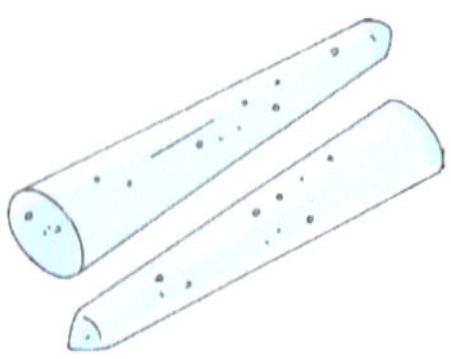 lk 

6.  ld 

7.  rt 

67. Cryptic Crossword

Decode the clues and fill the crossword with the homophones of the given clues.

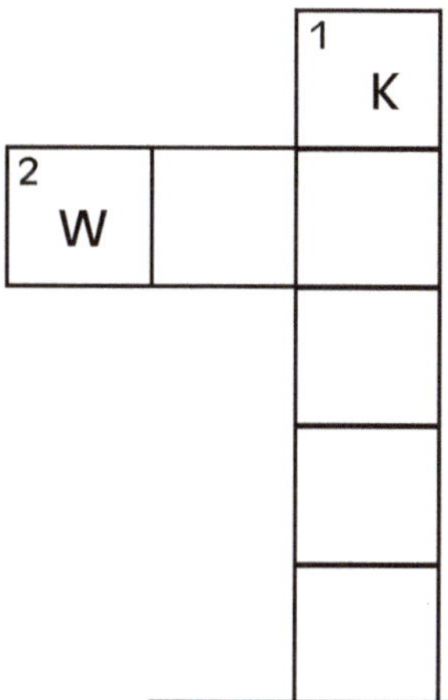

Down:

1. 

3. 4th

4. 

5. 

8. 8

Across:

2. 1

4. 

6. 

7. 

8. 

68. Choose It

Choose the correct homonym and complete the pair of sentences.

waves	nails	sink
bat	mine	bark

1. The tree has brown ________________.

   The dogs ______________ at night.

2. That car is _________________.

   He works in a coal ______________________.

3. There are ___________________ in the pond.

   She _________________ her hand.

4. The stones ____________________ in the water.

   Leave the plates in the _______________.

5. Hit the ball with the __________________.

   I saw a ________________ last night.

6. We should not bite our __________________.

   Hammer the _______________ in the wall.

69. Match Up

Read the words in each row and match them with the correct picture.

cub

cube

cup

coop

hug

huge

mud

mule

tub

tube

nut

news

cut

cute

70. Collective Nouns

Complete the crossword by filling in the collective nouns for the given clues.

Across:

1. _______ of cards
4. _______ of dancers
5. _______ of grapes
6. _______ of teachers
10. _______ of stars

Down:

2. _______ of sailors
3. _______ of flowers
7. _______ of soldiers
8. _______ of students
9. _______ of thieves

71. Words with 'C'

Words with hard and soft sounds of 'c' are hidden in the word search. Find and write them in the space below.

J	C	A	S	T	L	E	O	V	K
C	O	M	B	K	D	A	N	C	E
N	D	C	I	T	Y	C	X	F	G
M	O	Q	G	Z	L	F	A	C	E
X	J	D	C	O	N	E	H	Y	B
U	A	L	C	A	M	P	L	I	F
J	T	B	Z	G	C	A	R	E	U
I	J	R	O	P	E	N	C	I	L
C	E	U	Y	I	S	K	D	S	G
E	N	N	C	E	R	E	A	L	W
Z	S	B	C	E	L	E	R	Y	W
T	E	X	A	C	T	O	W	A	S

Words with soft 'c'	Words with hard 'c'

72. Recall and Tell

The pictures given below are from some famous stories. Identify and write their names.

1.

2.

3.

4.

5.

6.

Pinocchio	Little Red Riding Hood
Snow White	The Pied Piper
Rapunzel	Three Billy Goats

73. Find the Answer

Recall the poems you have read. Read the questions and match them to the answers.

1. Who scared little Miss Muffet?

2. What did the cow jump over?

3. Where did the pussy fell?

4. What thing did Jack and Jill want to fetch?

5. What shines like a diamond in the sky?

6. What is short and stout with a handle and a spout?

74. Word Game

Fill letters in the empty boxes such that two different but meaningful words are formed.

ug	ab	ar	op
st	in	sh	it

1.

S	P	I	N	C	H

2.

C	H			C	H

3.

P	L			L	Y

4.

D	U			E	M

5.

S	T			E	N

6.

D	E			C	H

7.

C	R			L	E

8.

R	U			U	T

75. Let's go Silent

The following words contain letters which are silent. Spell the words and circle the silent letter.

CASTLE

LAMB

COMB

ACHE

KNOCK

OFTEN

SIGN

ECHO

SCENE

COLUMN

KNEE

WRITE

HIGH

WRIST

SIGH

76. Chain of Events

Draw a line to match the event with the one which might happen after the given event.

1.	The sky is cloudy.	(a)	He knows all the answers.
2.	Today is Mary's Birth day.	(b)	He got poor marks in the test.
3.	John studied hard for the test.	(c)	It starts to rain.
4.	Mark missed the school bus.	(d)	She breaks the glass window.
5.	Zara kicked the football in the wrong direction.	(e)	She got a dress as a gift.
6.	Henry did not study for his test.	(f)	His father dropped him to the school.

77. Complete It

Some one skipped the silent letters while writing the following words. Complete the words by writing the missing letters.

CA_M

CLIM_

PAL_

DOU_T

_OUR

I_LAND

THUM_

_NIFE

_ONEST

YO_K

G_EST

RECEI_T

_NOT

PE_PLE

78. What Happens Next?

Assume the following events occur in your life. Write the possible outcome for each of the following.

1. Event: You lost your favourite book.

   Effect: ________________________________

   ____

2. Event: You forget your best friend's birthday.

   Effect: ________________________________

   ____

3. Event: You want to eat a cake.

   Effect: ________________________________

   ____

4. Event: You spilled the milk on the floor.

   Effect: ________________________________

   ____

5. Event: You have an exam tomorrow.

   Effect: ________________________________

   ____

79. The Ugly Duckling

See the picture and complete the passage given below.

Mother ________  has five ________ . Four eggs hatched into yellow ________ . Out of the fifth egg came a grey duckling. The other ducklings called him, 'An ugly duckling'. He became sad and ran away from ________ . One day he saw a beautiful ________  in the pond. She called him as a beautiful swan. He looked at his reflection in the ________ . He was not a duck. He was a beautiful swan.

80. Cause and Effect

Circle the possible cause of the following events.

1. There is a beautiful rainbow in the sky.

   It rained | It snowed

2. Jerry is very tired.

   He was sleeping | He was playing

3. Mandy got a beautiful gold medal.

   She scored zero | She won the quiz

4. There are puddles in the driveway.

   It rained heavily | It was sunny

5. Baby Tim is crying loudly.

   He is hungry | He is sleeping

6. The man has gained muscles.

   He went to school | He went to gym

7. He is angry at his friend.

   She told a lie | She offered help

81. The Clever Fox

One day a fox was sitting near a __________  . A __________  came and sat on the branch of the tree. The crow had a piece of _________  in its beak. The __________  was hungry but it could not climb the tree. It made a clever plan and said to the crow, 'Mr. Crow, you are a great singer. Why don't you sing a song?' On hearing this, the foolish crow opened its __________  to sing and dropped the apple. The fox grabbed the ________  and ran away.

82. Messy Maze

Follow the clues and help Ahna reach her house.

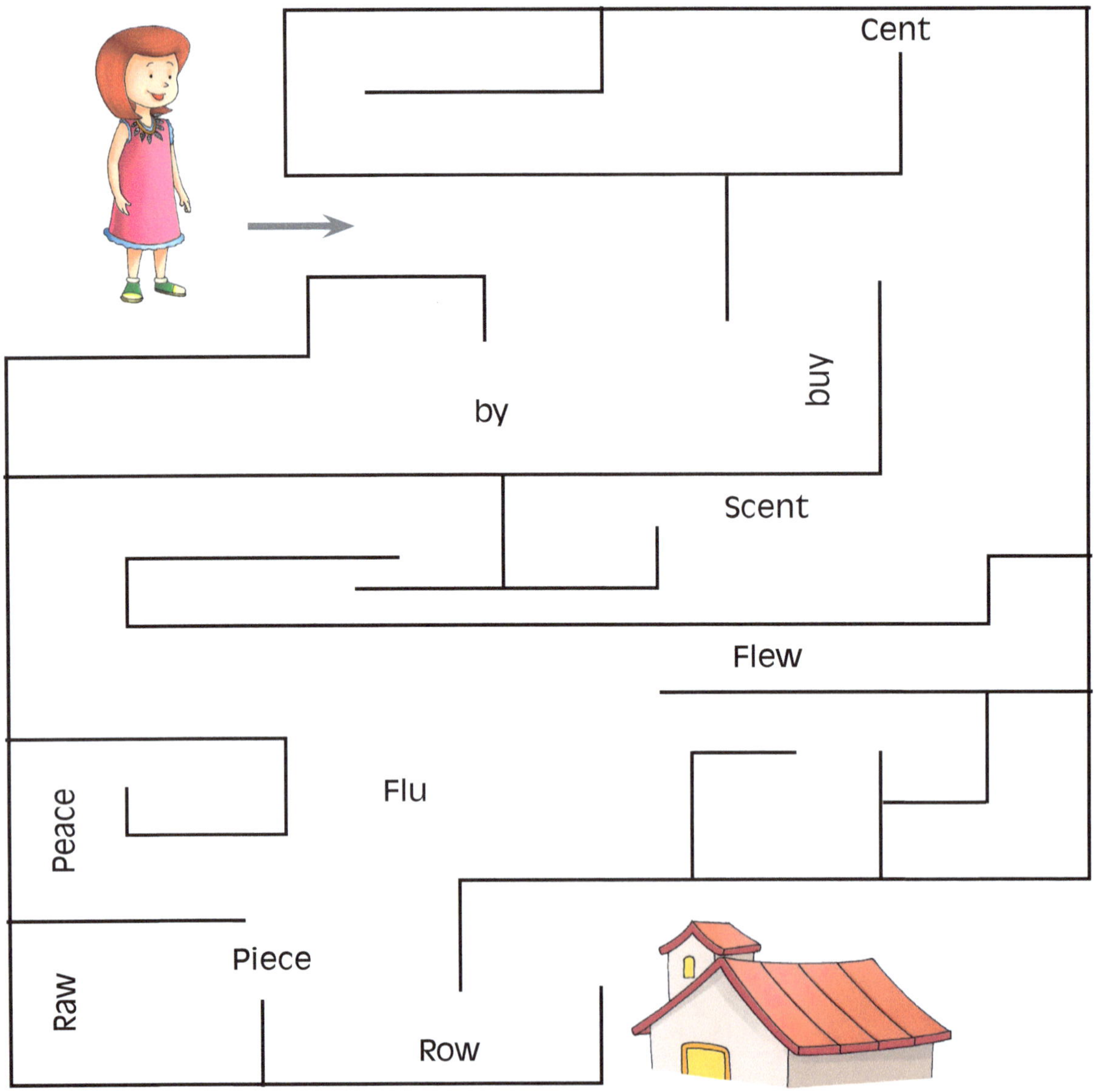

Clues:

1. I want to ________ a new dress.
2. This _________ smells very nice.
3. He has a bad __________.
4. Give me a __________ of cake.
5. ___________ the boat faster.

83. Puzzle Time

Read the clues and fill the crossword with words ending with letter 'e'.

Down:

1. Plural of mouse.
2. The home of a bear.
4. We talk to distant people using it.
5. The largest water creature.

Across:

3. A tool to sweep the garden.
4. A tree with needles.
6. an organ to smell with.
7. A 3-D model of Earth.

84. The Lion's Fear

Read the passage carefully and answer the questions given below.

There was a lion that feared nothing except the crowing of cocks. He used to shiver with fear on listening the crowing of cocks. He and the elephant were very good friends. One day the lion confessed his fear in front of the elephant. The elephant got shocked to hear what the lion said. He said to the lion "How can you be afraid of the crowing of cocks, I simply cannot understand." Just then a mosquito came there. The elephant got badly frightened that if the mosquito entered his ears he would be deaf. He started waving at the insect with his trunk. Now it was the lion that got a shock to see a giant animal being afraid of such a small mosquito.

1. What was lion afraid of?

   Lion was afraid of ______________________________.

2. Who was lion's friend?

   _______________________ was lion's friend.

3. What was elephant's reaction to lion's fear?

   He was ______________________________.

4. What frightened the elephant?

   A ______________________ frightened the elephant.

5. The opposite of good is _____________________.

6. The opposite of small is _____________________.

7. Name a thing or person you are afraid of.

   ____

85. Some Clever Mice

Read the passage carefully and answer the questions given below.

Once there lived a greedy cat. She loved to eat almost anything but eating a nice fat mouse was her favourite. There were many of them in her master's house. She used to catch one for breakfast, one for lunch and one for dinner every day. After few days when the mice noticed their number decreasing rapidly, they got worried. They were very frightened to move out of their holes for the fear of getting caught by the cat. They sat inside the hole and kept watching if the cat was around. In this way, the cat could not get any mouse to eat. She began to get hungry, so finally she thought of a trick. She fell down in front of the mice's hole so that the mice could see her. She gave a little meow and lay flat still, pretending to be dead. But none of the mouse came out. So after waiting for a while, she whispered "I am dead. You can come out now." But the mouse replied "We are not stupid as you. We can tell the difference between a live cat and a dead cat."

1. What did the cat loves to eat?
   The cat loves to eat a ________________.
2. How many mice did the cat eat every day?
   The cat ate ____________ mice every day.
3. Where did the mice hide from the cat?
   The mice hid in their ______________.
4. What did the cat do to catch the mouse?
   The cat pretended to be _______________.
5. Who was clever in the story?
   The _______________ were clever in the story.
6. The opposite of love is ________________.
7. The opposite of stupid is ________________.

86. Word Jumble

Words with hard and soft sounds of 'g' are hidden in the word search. Find and write them in the space below.

P	J	A	M	L	G	E	R	M	L
G	G	Y	B	D	R	A	G	O	N
R	I	G	O	A	T	A	S	Q	Y
N	G	A	N	G	I	F	T	S	H
H	X	B	I	G	O	P	A	G	E
E	D	P	G	N	S	J	L	R	D
S	G	Y	A	N	G	E	L	S	O
O	R	A	N	G	E	C	P	K	N
C	M	Y	E	N	E	R	G	Y	R
G	U	L	R	G	O	A	L	Q	R
A	H	O	G	Q	Q	G	E	M	S
P	I	K	U	O	I	Y	R	S	V

Words with soft 'g'	Words with hard 'g'

87. Summer Season

The picture below shows summer season. Mark the objects which should not be in the picture.

Circle the clothes that you wear in summer.

88. Eat and Tell

Circle the food items that you eat in summers.

Circle the food items which taste sweet.

Answers

1. Match It
1. Grassland 2. Polar region
3. Desert 4. Ocean
5. Rainforest 6. Lake

2. Word Search
1. No Smoking 2. Do not Touch
3. No Parking 4. Radioactive
5. Handicapped 6. Fire Exit
7. Restaurant 8. No Entry

3. Animal Produce
1. Hen 2. Cow
3. Fish 4. Sheep
5. Bees

4. Foody Crossword
Across: Down:
2. Pineapple 1. Onion
3. Orange 4. Garlic
6. Cherry 5. Peas
8. Peach 7. Radish

6. Pollutants
Sewage, Industries, Fossil fuel, Chemical, Litter, Pesticide, Nuclear, Automobile

7. Correct the Sequence
1. Digging soil 2. Sowing seed
3. Watering 4. Put in Sunlight
5. Sapling 6. Plant

8. Growing Patterns
1.  2. 
3. 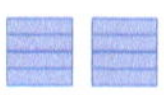 4.
5.  6. 

9. Plants as Givers
Apple, Kiwi
Carrot, Spinach
Cotton, Jute
Mustard, Sunflower
Wheat, Rice

10. Life of a Frog
1. Eggs 2. Tadpole
3. Tadpole with legs 4. froglet
5. Adult frog 6. skin
7. land, water 8. webbed
9. long

11. Speller's Zone
1. Calendar 2. Column
3. Argument 4. Further
5. Lollipop 6. Interrupt
7. Tomorrow 8. Publicly

12. Name It
1. Utensils 2. Tools
3. Scissor 4. Stationery
5. Brush 6. Water hose

14. My Senses
1. Hear 2. See
3. Smell 4. Taste
5. Touch

15. Mirror Image
1.  2. 
3.  4. 
5.  6. 
7.  8. 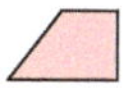

16. Take me Home
1. Kennel 2. Stable
3. Shed 4. Coop
5. Fish Bowl 6. Cage

17. Tricky Phrases
1. Sit on the fence
2. A piece of cake
3. Put a sock in it
4. A bird in hand is worth two in the bush
5. The last laugh
6. A drop in the ocean
7. A shot in the arm
8. Forgive and forget

18. Find the Sign
1. stop 2. walk
3. cross 4. left turn
5. prohibits 6. u-turn
7. roundabout

19. Bird Riddles
1. Penguin 2. Ostrich
3. Cock 4. Owl
5. Parrot 6. Eagle

20. Unscramble the Words
1. Windy 2. Thunder
3. Cloudy 4. Sunny
5. Rainy 6. Snowy
7. Partly cloudy

21. Pollution Panic
1. smoke 2. factories
3. music 4. waste
5. Deforestation 6. chemicals
7. spills

22. Water Cycle
1. Sun shines
2. Evaporation
3. Condensation
4. Rainfall

23. Finish the Patterns
1.  2. 
3. # 4. 
5.  6.
7.  8. 

24. Being a Butterfly
1. egg, leaves
2. caterpillar, eggshell

3. pupa
4. butterfly

25. Hard to Spell

1. Weird
2. Siege
3. Receive
4. Piece
5. Friend
6. Foreign
7. Believe
8. Achieve
9. Height
10. Science

26. Who Am I?

1. chef
2. doctor
3. plumber
4. teacher
5. soldier

29. Find It

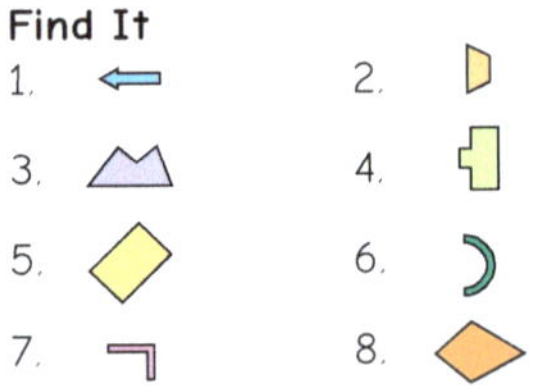

30. Where Are They?

1. Between
2. Below
3. Inside
4. Bottom
5. Above
6. Over
7. Behind
8. Under

32. Guess the Animal

1. Meerkat
2. Snail
3. Fox
4. Polar bear
5. Tiger
6. Elephant

35. Word Scramble

1. Swing
2. Sneeze
3. Scrub
4. Shout
5. Skate
6. Stand
7. Swim
8. Slide

37. Double It

1. Button
2. Teddy
3. Puppy
4. Muffin
5. Pillow
6. Carrot

38. Ride It

Across:
2. Bus
5. Aeroplane
7. Bicycle
8. Rocket

Down:
1. Submarine
3. Ship
4. Sledge
6. Car
9. Train

41. Race Time

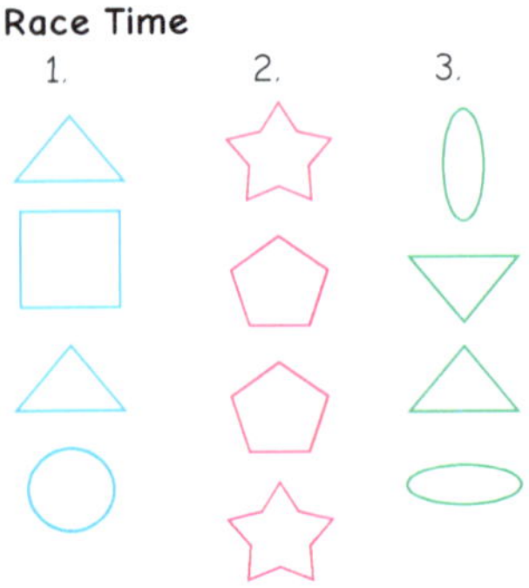

42. Visiting Places

1. Hotel
2. Library
3. School
4. Market
5. Museum
6. Bank
7. Hospital
8. Park

43. Find the Pattern

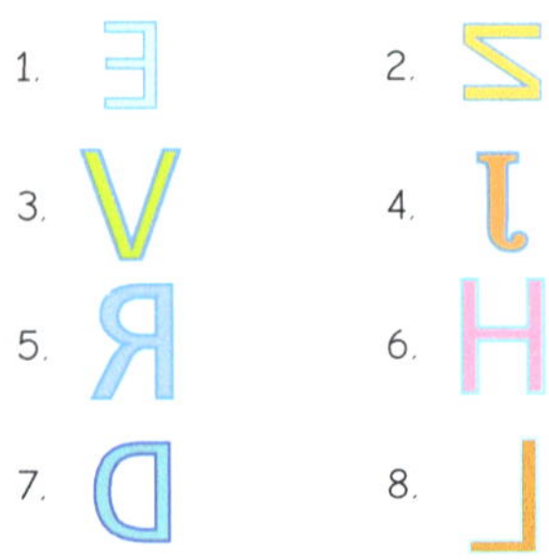

44. Word Clues

1. C
2. O
3. U
4. R
5. A
6. G
7. E

45. What's that Animal?

1. Fowl
2. Zebra
3. Hare
4. Horse
5. Bear
6. Owl
7. Deer
8. Echidna

46. Prefix Time

1. Rewrite, Replay, Rebuild
2. Uncut, Unlock, Unhappy
3. Superman, Superglue, Superstar

47. Crazy Colours

1. Z-Red
2. Queen-Green
3. Cottage-Orange
4. Track-Black
5. Pilot-Violet
6. Night-White
7. Ink-Pink
8. Screw-Blue

48. Bake a Cake

1. rainy
2. cake
3. apron, waist
4. bake
5. grapes
6. plate
7. tray

49. Finding Sounds

1. Wheel
2. King
3. Teeth
4. Torch
5. Sheep
6. Duck
7. Phone

50. Words Fusion

1. Lunchbox
2. Rainbow
3. Lighthouse
4. Fishbowl
5. Toothbrush
6. Popcorn
7. Sunflower

51. Word Find

1. R
2. E
3. A
4. D
5. I
6. N
7. G

52. Suffix Time

1. Drawing, Sleeping, Cooking
2. Readable, Washable, Laughable
3. Mouthful, Fearful, Spoonful

53. Rhyme Time

Hat-Bat　Tie-Eye
Pants-Ants　Dress-Chess

Answers

Sock-Clock Coat-Remote

Vest-Nest

55. Consonant Cluster

1. CL 2. SW 3. BL
4. PL 5. CL 6. IN
7. RO

56. Match-Making

1. Butterfly 2. Cupcake
3. Goldfish 4. Baseball
5. Notebook 6. Earring
7. Snowman 8. Teapot
9. Windmill 10. Scarecrow

57. Name It

1. Beat 2. Scare
3. Pat 4. Asleep
5. Grab 6. Recall
7. Slip 8. Share

58. Word Mania

1. A 2. W 3. E 4. S
5. O 6. M 7. E

59. In a Fix

1. Childish 2. Uncle
3. Unwell 4. Rainy
5. Training 6. Planet
7. Ugly 8. Washing

60. Foody Fun

Cherry-Berry Plum-Drum
Carrot-Parrot Pea-Sea
Fig-Twig Pear-Bear
Corn-Horn

62. Pick the Sound

1. gr 2. tr 3. pr
4. br 5. cr 6. fr
7. dr

63. Guess the Word

1. flower 2. pale
3. hole 4. knot
5. steel 6. deer
7. tail

64. Name the Group

1. Herd 2. Colony
3. Swarm 4. Pack
5. Floor 6. School
7. Pride 8. Litter

65. Pick One

1. Robot 2. Frog
3. Bone 4. Soap
5. Log 6. Mop

66. Circle It

1. Gift 2. Tent
3. Lamp 4. Pink
5. Chalk 6. Child
7. Shirt

67. Cryptic Crossword

Across:
2. Won
4. Stares
6. Hare
7. Male
9. Blew

Down:
1. Knight
3. Forth
4. Son
5. Sell
8. Ate

68. Choose It

1. bark 2. mine
3. waves 4. sink
5. bat 6. nails

71. Words with 'C'

1. city, pencil, dance, face, celery, cereal
2. camp, care, castle, comb, exact, cone

72. Recall and Tell

1. Snow white
2. Rapunzel
3. Three billy goats
4. The Pied piper
5. Little red riding hood
6. Pinocchio

73. Find the Answer

1. Spider 2. Moon
3. Well 4. Pail of water
5. Star 6. Teapot

74. Word Game

1. Spin, Inch 2. Chit, Itch
3. Plug, Ugly 4. Dust, Stem
5. Stop, Open 6. Dear, Arch
7. Crab, Able 8. Rush, Shut

75. Let's go Silent

Lamb Comb
Castle Knock
Ache Sign
Scene Echo
High Knee
Write Often
Column Sign
Wrist

76. Chain of Events

1. c 2. e 3. a
4. f 5. d 6. b

77. Complete It

Calm	Climb	Palm
Hour	Doubt	Island
Thumb	Knife	Honest
Yolk	Guest	Receipt
Knot	People	

79. The Ugly Duckling

duck, eggs, ducklings, home, swan, water

80. Cause and Effect

1. It rained
2. He was playing
3. She won the quiz
4. It rained heavily
5. He is hungry
6. He went to gym
7. She told a lie

81. The Clever Fox

tree, crow, apple, fox, beak, apple

82. Messy Maze

1. buy 2. scent
3. flu 4. piece
5. Row

83. Puzzle Time

Across:	Down:
3. Rake	1. Mice
4. Pine	2. Cave
6. Nose	4. Phone
7. Globe	5. Whale

84. The Lion's Fear

1. crowing of cocks
2. Elephant
3. shocked
4. mosquito
5. bad
6. big

85. Some Clever Mice

1. fat mouse
2. three
3. holes
4. dead
5. mice
6. hate
7. clever

86. Word Jumble

1. page, germ, orange, angel, energy, gem
2. dragon, goat, goal, gift, big, gang